Choices that we make are
what we are made of!

ISBN: 9798473961034

I Am Oweta's Daughter

Beverly Ross

My mom was a loving woman. Her love was steadfast and never failing! For months, now, I have been contemplating about my next book I would publish. I looked deep within my inspirations in life. Why is it, I had a great life, a great mom, a fantastic dad, and grew up in an awesome Christian home and I am so drawn to help hurting and broken people? As I thought about all the broken people, who have lost their way, I came to the realization, all my inspiration and who I became, started with my loving mom! She was my angel who loved me and protected me by covering me with the wings of a Savior who was her best friend. I am different from my mom in so many ways, but I think she put all the best of herself in me.

My mom and I were close, and I so longed to be a mother. I loved having a mom who taught me the values of motherhood. We began feeling we would be childless, and I had prayed God would give us a child. One night, God woke me up and His words were: "You're going to have a baby!" I was so excited and woke Mike up to tell him! He probably thought I was crazy, but I knew God's voice and it happened just as He said. Eighteen months after Bryan was born, God blessed us with a second son, Kevin. We are blessed to have them both in our lives!

In this book, I will share with you many things about my mom that created in me a heart that loves and respects my Lord and Savior Jesus Christ. I will share with you how she was a teacher who not only taught me but allowed me to step out on my own and take steps without judging me. She cheered me when she approved of my ways, and always showed her love, even if I was off course! I will share with you how she handled so many obstacles that came against her in her health. I will share with you how she handled some very harsh losses in her life and how many of her fears held her back. I will also share with you how even in her fears, she let me go, and trusted me to make good choices! She was always encouraging me! She was my Sunday School teacher! She was my strong tower! She was my biggest fan! She birthed love in me and then set me free in the world to spread it around! So, as you read, "I Am Oweta's Daughter," let her sweetness soften your hurts and lift your spirits to a new level. Author- Beverly Ross

Dedications

- To my brothers, Gary and Dennis, who also shared the love of this special lady!

- To my dad, whose love for my mom, was a portrait of the love that Jesus Christ has for His church. He studied in his Bible daily and taught his children to love and serve God. He was a dedicated husband and provider for this tender and special lady.

- To my mom's sister, Carolyn, who has served in Mom's place as a second mom all my life. The love between all of us has been beautiful!

- To all those who loved and met my mom and sometimes call her an angel! She loved and impacted many in her quiet home. All who visited, knew they were loved!

- To all those hurting, who didn't have a mother and to those who had a mother but didn't feel loved by her!

- To LaDonna Cook, my brother's daughter, whose faith has held her through her illness.

- To my sister-in-law, Cindy, who helped me with edits and my sister-in-law Sandy, who encouraged me to put my writings into a book. And my dearest friend Jeanne, who read and looked for final edits.

Table of Contents

CHAPTER 1

My Mom.... A Worthy Woman

Not a day goes by that I don't miss Mom and Dad. She never wanted Daddy to go home to Heaven before her, but it happened. It was so sad to see Dad having kidney failure, a major stroke and prostate cancer after many years of suffering from crippling arthritis. The arthritis was in his hands and feet from the time he was very young. He was a survivor. During his kidney dialysis, they put in a stint which they feel caused an infection. This caused him to have a mitral valve regurgitation of his heart. He was not a candidate for surgery. It happened in January 2007 and by October 2007, he died.

Mom always told me the story of when I was very young. I was just a toddler. My

Dad had served in the Coast Guard and after coming back, was in the VA hospital because of his arthritis. Mom said I had a little telephone and would pretend to talk to him on the phone.

My dad, the Coast Guard single man, was so in love with this lady! He always referred to her as darling in his letters. He had one goal and one goal only! To get out of the Coast Guard, go back to Texas, and ask this beautiful lady for her hand in marriage! Of course, he knew he had to ask her dad for her hand in marriage first!

While sitting at a family reunion, celebrating one of their last anniversaries together, I'll never forget the way Dad and Mom laughed as they told their stories. Dad talked about having a giant fishhook, and he knew how much Mom's dad loved to fish. He giggled at the reunion, when he told the story about coming back from the Coast Guard, getting to her dad's house in Texas, and approaching him about marrying his daughter. He took the big fishhook and asked if he could give him the fishhook in exchange for marrying his daughter. I remember Mom's laughter and joy, as she listened to Dad's story from so long ago! I had never heard him tell it before!

Mom held onto everything! Her things were her treasures! Especially the letters that Dad sent her all through the days he served on the Coast Guard ship. After their deaths, I ran across the box of letters. I think it took me two days to read them. They took me on a journey of two people in love. The journey of a man, who loved and respected a woman so much, he knew he had to be the perfect man for this perfect girl. He couldn't wait to come home to her and make her his bride! He saw her perfection as being a strong Christian woman and he didn't see himself being ready for her, until he too could find what she had. He said in his letters, he knew there were things he had to change, and he was working on it. I really loved the way he was seeing his need for change, to be special for her. He wanted to be close to God first and he wanted to take care of a few things to prepare to marry her. My dad did just that! He got it right with God. He sought to follow God and serve him as a personal Savior.

My mom expected good things from people! Her love for God reflected a love to others that made them want to have what she had. Wow! I wanted that to be in me! She caused me to feel that way about people. She looked through hard times and saw hope for change! She lived through fears and talked about them, but she always encouraged me to be strong! She lived through sickness, and yet she never let that sickness make her bitter or mad, nor did she blame God for not healing her while here on this earth. She is healed now and kept her eyes on her heavenly home. She held tightly to the promise that when she went to Heaven, there would be no more sickness, no more pain, and she would be with her wonderful Savior, Jesus Christ for ever and ever!

Mom was in her living room one day when she was about forty-nine or so. I had recently married and moved away. Dad's job moved him to a new location where he was an operator in the plant. They moved to one of the plant houses nearby. It had a long living room, so Mom sat in a chair at one end. She looked up toward the front door, and there she saw Jesus coming in.

He walked over to her, hugged her, and said, "Oweta, I just want to tell you I love you!" Then He went away.

A year or so after that, I was talking with Mom on the phone. They had moved back into their house in town and had left the plant house. While talking, Mom suddenly went silent. I could hear noises, but she wouldn't answer me. It really scared me! I didn't know what to do! I called a neighbor down the street and asked her if she could go check on my mom. Mom had gone into a seizure. At first, they were petit mal seizures, but there were times she had grand mal seizures. We were blessed the medications made them milder. Mom always felt that Jesus knew what she would be facing the next few years of her life, and he came to her that day to comfort her and let her know He was there with her and would never leave her side. He walked with her, through the hard times. She carried that memory of being held by Him.

Mom always told me the story of when she was a little girl. She had climbed up on the cabinets and fell off. She cut her head badly and they were unable to take her in for medical attention. She was told that often a fall when you are young can cause seizures later in life, so she thought that was why her seizures started.

Dad died October 6, 2007. The day after Daddy's funeral, Mom and I were heading back home. We had to bury him about twelve hours away from our current homes, so the trip was long. It was right after we got home, I saw Mom have one of her last seizures.

When Mom and Dad's health began declining, it was necessary to move them closer to us. I was a realtor and found them one home, so they could move out of their two homes. They had one home on Lake Kemp, about four hours away from our childhood home. They chose to keep both homes and, in the winter, stayed at our childhood home. When weather permitted, they lived at the lake.

Mom just couldn't have things at the lake and things at home. Each time they packed all her things and hauled them back and forth. Dad would lecture her about taking so much and say, "Oweta, why don't you just keep what you need here at the lake, and we won't have to load so much." Mom just wouldn't have it that way. Dad served her needs and saw to it she was content whenever they would travel. He gave her that freedom.

Wherever they lived, the doctors they saw were 50 miles from them. As the health issues started, they stayed more at the lake, so they could be near the doctors there. Dad had been diagnosed with prostate cancer and he had to go in for surgery. After surgery, we were about to take him home and I asked them if they had walked him at all. They had not. A newer nurse came in and decided he needed to walk. She didn't realize how weak he was and walked him with my older brother Gary by his side, down the long hall. It was there, he had a major stroke and we almost lost him. Gary caught him on the way down. I felt guilty over that for quite a while, wondering if I should have suggested the walk. Possibly though, I realized that had he had that stroke with us, he would have died.

Mom suffered many falls caused by the seizures. In one of the falls, she fractured her vertebrae and later, in another fall, she broke her hip. With the hospital being 50 miles from the lake, I would go stay with them each time through the illnesses. If Dad was in the hospital, daily, Mom and I would drive to see him and come home at night. If Mom was in the hospital, Dad and I would do the same. I know there was always high stress during those times.

During one of Dad's stays in the intensive care unit, Mom and I spent many hours in the lobby. Dad had undergone prostate surgery and experienced a large blood loss resulting in transfusions. I embroidered a whole set of cup towels in that lobby during that time. We met a sweet Korean nurse who worked in the unit. Mom and I were heading back to see Daddy. The double doors had a button you pushed to go back to the Intensive Care unit, and we pushed the button. Just about the time we pushed it, the double doors opened, and the Korean nurse was at the doors, coming out, and my mom's pants fell to the ground. Her elastic wasn't tight enough to hold them up! The little nurse was so sweet! My mom was so embarrassed! We all began to giggle and talk. The nurse shared with us how she had to stand in long lines in her country at one time and just didn't make it to the bathroom. She shared her embarrassment with Mom, and she was one of the lady's mom allowed to feel her love. She had a way of making you feel loved. Her love had a personal feel to it! Mom's giggles during that time were priceless to me!

Mom also suffered from tachycardia. This would mean her heart would beat rapidly. She had issues with that and sometimes it would put her in the hospital. During one of those episodes, she had her chance to beat Daddy to Heaven. She went into cardiac arrest, and they had to shock her five times to revive her. By the time I got there, she was so mad! Not only did they stop her trip to Heaven, but they left her in great pain and bruised her. She never wanted that to happen again! At the end of her life, it was her heart that took her home.

I loved my parents. I remember when Mom was able to fish with Dad and she loved it. She didn't like to travel because she would get car sick, so she would take a bottle of Dramamine pills with her. Otherwise on Dad's trips to California and Oregon, she would have been throwing up all the way. She loved visiting the family when we traveled, but just getting there was the problem.

She loved serving you in her home. She loved to cook. Some of her famous recipes were her chocolate chip cookies, her doughnuts (spread all over the counters), her fried chicken, and her mashed potatoes. She and her mom canned dill pickles and other things, so she loved to be in her kitchen. When Mom began losing her balance and ability to stand, Dad, the loving man that he was, took over the cooking. He served her with so much commitment to make life easier for her. He felt she was worthy of his love. To any man reading this book, be sure your special lady feels worthy to be loved by you and have your support in her life.

My dad was a great symbol of a godly man and the way he took care of his bride. Mom on the other hand thought at times his temperamental way of saying things was a bit cruel and hurt her feelings. Marriages are not perfect, but with God and His word rooted in our relationships, we can build on a firm foundation and keep our lives and happiness in good perspective.

We had an awesome 50th anniversary celebration for Dad and Mom. We had a large cake made for them and invited many friends and family to attend. I remember one of Mom's long-lost friends had heard about it and showed up. Mom and I were outside the hall when she showed up. As Mom and her began talking, I suddenly heard Mom say, "So you're the one who put dog food under our bed sheets!"

They begin to laugh! We had a great time celebrating their 50th anniversary. We found the pastor who had married them 50 years before, and they restated their vows to each other with him doing the ceremony. My brothers walked Mom in, and I walked in with Dad. The minister's sweet wife played piano for everyone, and my brothers, sisters-in-law, and other family members did some music for them. My nephew, Glenn wrote this song for them about their life:

Won't You Pray by Glenn Cook

(verse 1)

Sitting around the dinner

table, about to eat the

food Oweta had

prepared, with the

sustenance of her love an

aroma of a tender heart

filled with strength and

kindness to one hungry

soul, a meal garnished

with her smile would say,

"Amis, won't you pray?"

(Chorus)

Our most gracious heavenly Father, We're
so grateful to you

For your many

blessings, for our

home and family too

Keep your hand upon

us and save those

grandkids too.

As we thank you for the food and the fish
we caught today.

(verse 2)

Sittin' in Grandpa's truck, getting ready to
go

from the lake Amis brought us

to with that enduring kind of

love an approval like no other

man I know filled with

experience of trial

An example of an overcoming soul- would
take off his hat and say, "Oweta won't
you pray?"

CHAPTER 2
A Letter from God

My mom was a stay-at-home mom. She used to love to drive and she would drive all the time! She loved being able to carpool, taking her kids and others to school. She loved taking her mom grocery shopping, and they would go from store to store, looking for the bargains so they could save money. Her mom did not drive, so it was a joy for Mom to be with her during these times. Because she was not having seizures in her early years, she loved being there for her mom. Later in life, when the seizures hit, she had to give up driving to keep other people safe. I remember being with her one day and she had a seizure at a stop sign. I had to encourage her at that time that driving was just not safe! I knew that if she hurt someone, due to having a seizure while driving, she would never forgive herself.

One time, before her seizures began, a little boy pulled out in front of her on a bicycle and she hit him. He had shot out from between cars and she didn't have time to avoid him. Even though he was not severely hurt, she was haunted by what could have happened and felt so responsible for it.

Because I encouraged her to quit driving, she did. This meant that now she would depend on me, Dad, or someone else to be her driver. She spent a lot of time at home and always found things to keep her busy or happy. I don't remember hearing her complain, because she had lost the important things in her life like driving. Instead, she focused on being an encouragement to anyone who came to see her, and she found a great love in watching Christian television. She knew the people on the Christian shows, and she knew their stories and they became somewhat of a family to her. When they hurt or had a loss, she felt their pain as though it was a family member. She loved their music and knew all the Gaither's songs and their singers. She is now in Heaven worshipping with many of the people she knew from the TV, as though they were her own family. I know when I get to Heaven, she will be so excited to introduce me to them.

During the times she was at home and living through her illnesses, she found a very close relationship with God, as He was her personal Savior and she knew He would never leave her or forsake her, NO MATTER WHAT! It was during one of those times, she wrote a letter about a message she felt God gave her. My niece, LaDonna, is Mom's oldest granddaughter. She is my oldest brother, Gary's daughter.

LaDonna suffered from mental illness and it has been very difficult to go through. We have seen God's healing working in her life and won't stop believing till she is completely healed! It is so important to LaDonna, to get the words of this letter out to anyone who might need to hear them. This letter has been a blessing to her! I feel that this book will be a vehicle to making this happen, so this is the letter from God, given to my mother, Oweta Cook.

My dearest child, I love you! I shed my own blood for you, to make you clean. You are new, so believe it is true! You are lovely in my eyes and I created you just as you are. Do not criticize yourself or get down for not being perfect in your own eyes. This leads only to frustration. I want you to trust me, my child. One step, one day at a time. Dwell in my power and love and be free to be yourself! Don't allow other people to run over you. I will guide you if you will let me. Be aware of my presence in everything. I give you patience, love, joy, and peace. Look to me for answers. I am your Shepherd and I will lead you, follow me only! Do not forget this! Listen! I will tell you my will for your life.

Do you understand? I love you, my child. Let it flow from you. Spill over to all you touch. Be not concerned with yourself. You are my responsibility! I will change you without you hardly knowing it! You are to love yourself and love others, simply because I love you! Take your eyes off yourself! Look only at me. I lead! I change! I mold! But not when you are trying! I won't fight your efforts! You are mine! Let me have the joy of making you like Christ. Let me love you! Let me give you happiness! Peace! Joy! Health! No one else can. You see my child; you are not your own. You have been bought with blood. Now, you belong to me. It is really none of your business how I deal with you. Your only command is to look to me! Never to yourself! Never to others! Do not struggle, fight, rebel but relax in my love! Do not worry! Just trust me! I know what is best and will do it in you. Now, I need for you to allow me to love you freely! My will is perfect! My love is sufficient! I will supply your needs! For I love you!

Your Heavenly Father

Jesus was telling my mom in the letter He gave her, that no matter what she was going through, He was there with her;

walking with her, talking with her, guiding and directing her life. He would be everything she needed and always be there for her. The same is true for you! Jesus wants a walking, talking relationship with you. He paid the price for your sins when He died on the cross and He is a friend who will stick closer to you than a brother. He is the friend who will never leave you or forsake you.

Mom taught me from the time I was a child, sitting in her School class. My friend, Jeanne, laughs and says that one time she brought her full-size baby doll to Mom's Sunday school class and Mom counted her as a student. Moms that care, teach you that Jesus cares! Moms that don't care, probably never had a mom that taught them about the love of Jesus! If your mom had no knowledge or relationship with Jesus, then forgive her! Jesus never stops trying to reach the lost and His Word will get to you one way or another, even if it's through the stories of my mom, Oweta, who taught me so much about Jesus. I hope her stories will teach you too!

CHAPTER 3
My Mom Believed in Angels

I know people often said, that my mom was an angel. She, however, knew who angels were. As a young girl, my mom had a special plate that hung on the wall. On that special plate was a picture of a wobbly bridge, with a huge angel and a young boy and a young girl. Mom would always tell me the story about the angel, and how we were assigned angels to watch over us every day of our lives. She explained to me that the angel standing over the children, was there to look after them and protect them as they crossed the wobbly old bridge.

I remember loving the story and many times I would ask Mom to tell it to me again, and she always would. She knew that she, herself, was not an angel, and taught me who angels really were. I believe people call her an angel, because of her love and protective spirit she had over watching those she loved! It's a blessing that she was seen that way. She knew the angels were sent here to the earth to look out for God's children. She told me the angels were assigned to each of us. They would protect us when we were in danger. Not only are angels God's protectors, they are messengers. Remember God used his angels to announce the virgin birth of Jesus. Before that, an angel came to Zachariah.

(Luke 1:13-20), says, "13 But the angel said to him: "Do not be afraid, Zechariah; your prayer has been heard. Your wife Elizabeth will bear you a son, and you are to call him John. 14 He will be a joy and delight to you, and many will rejoice because of his birth, 15 for he will be great in the sight of the Lord. He is never to take wine or other fermented drink, and he will be filled with the Holy Spirit even before he is born. 16 He will bring back many of the people of Israel to the Lord their God. 17 And he will go on before the Lord, in the spirit and power of

Elijah, to turn the hearts of the parents to their children and the disobedient to the wisdom of the righteous—to make ready a people prepared for the Lord." 18 Zechariah asked the angel, "How can I be sure of this? I am an old man and my wife is well along in years."

19 The angel said to him, "I am Gabriel. I stand in the presence of God, and I have been sent to speak to you and to tell you this good news. 20 And now you will be silent and not able to speak until the day this happens, because you did not believe my words, which will come true at their appointed time."

It happened just as the angel said! I believe angels are also sent here to guide us to our eternal heavenly home, after we pass from this earth. You will see accounts of this in the Bible. One passage in:

(Luke 16-22), "22 "The time came when the beggar died, and the angels carried him to

Abraham's side. The rich man also died and was buried."

When Mom died, it had only been about three months after we lost dad. We only lived about two miles from where she and Dad lived. Because of Mom's health, I knew I had to move her in with us. We got all her things ready, and made room at our house to move her in. She had a brass bed which she loved. She had her special mattress, and we loaded it all up carefully. We left Mom at her house, and I followed Mike, as he had the mattress in the truck and all her bedding. Because we weren't going far, Mike had not secured everything down very well. Suddenly, out of the back of the truck flew her mattress and her bed all over the road. I gasped! I knew how distraught Mom would be, after losing Dad, and now her mattress was going to be destroyed! And her brass bed! To our amazement, nothing got damaged. We never told Mom about that incident. We put everything back in the truck, tied it down, and proceeded to the house. I had to eventually put Mom's hospital bed into the room, as she had to be in it as her health grew worse. About three months later, it was evident that Mom wouldn't be with us for very long. Her heart was not doing well.

It was the night of her death, right at the end of December. Dad passed away October 6, 2007. My brother and sister-in-law had come to be with us, and Mom's sister was on the way with her husband. My sister-in-law, Sandy and my brother Gary were asleep in the other room the night she died. I slept in the room with Mom. She was in the hospital bed and I was on her brass bed. The first time I woke up, I noticed her arm was hanging off the bed, but I didn't realize that she was gone. A few seconds later I checked her, and she was gone.

My sister-in-law who was in the other room, was awakened by the swoosh of angel wings. She said she knew when she heard it, that Mom was gone. It was a very comforting feeling for her to know that the angels had taken Mom to her heavenly home. Death can be very hard, but when you know the person you love is no longer in pain, and when you know the person you love, knows Jesus and could not wait to be with Him, it's much easier to let them go.

Before they took Mom, we all gathered around her bed and sang an old song called, "I'll Meet You in The Morning." It was our way of saying goodbye, and our way to celebrate her trip to her heavenly home with joy. They came to get her and carried her out on the stretcher. They sent a man and a little tiny lady, not realizing we had very steep stairs to go down. My brother Gary walked out with Mom as they carried her down. The little lady almost dropped Mom on her end, but my brother was able to help them catch her.

Months later, I was on my computer looking at a computer picture done by Google Earth.

Mom died around Christmas time, and that was the only year we put up luminary lights down the sidewalk. As I was looking at Google Earth and going around our house, there were the luminary lights going down our sidewalk. In our driveway was my brother's white van. I knew it was the day Mom died. My brother was here one night only.

My thoughts were, "Oh my! It's a wonder they didn't catch them taking Mom down our steps and almost dropping her."

I had to laugh! I know it's kind of strange, but in a way, that was comforting to me, to know that God provided a picture of that day even if it was done by Google Earth. It was His way of saying I was there, and I cared. That old body wasn't my mom any longer! She flew off with the angels.

The Bible says we also at times entertain angels unaware! In:

(Hebrews 13:2), The Bible tells us, do not forget to show hospitality to strangers, for by so doing some people have shown hospitality to angels without knowing it.

Angels can take human form. In one instance of my life, I believe that happened. Perhaps other times as well. Mom taught me to enjoy motherhood! She told me not to expect her to be my babysitter! She wanted to enjoy being a grandma! She loved kids but wanted me to be a responsible mother. If I worked, it was my job to hire and pay a sitter! I chose to babysit other people's kids, so I could be home with my boys. Leaving them with strangers was just not for me!

We were in a small town when the boys were young. Dad and Mom lived on the other end of town from us. As the boys were older, they would always go visit Grandpa and Grandma on their bicycles. Dad and Mom loved having them and they were always welcome. Dad was hands on with them. As they got older, they even went on vacations with them. But Mom taught me to be their mother!

It was one of those hard days, when it seemed like everything that could go wrong was going wrong. I remember being very upset with Mike, probably over finances. I had a visor on my car that had broken. I decided that day that the boys and I would drive to the local salvage yard twelve miles away, to look through the wrecked cars. I didn't want to buy a new visor, so I went there to look for a visor that was still in good condition.

On the way there, the boys used to sing with me. I taught them how to sing harmony as well as lead. They both have good voices. I remember as we were singing my heart was sad, but we kept on singing! I was enjoying being with the boys.

When we got to the salvage yard, it was strange that there was a long line at the front desk. This is not a real big town, and the salvage yard is never that busy! As we were standing in line, in front of us there was a very handsome and very tall gentleman. He turned around and looked down at the boys. He began to talk to us and to them. I remember him saying, "I bet you look a lot like your daddy".

His voice was very kind and soothing. I didn't understand why he made me feel so much better as we talked. Suddenly, he said he forgot something in his car. He took off, and he never came back. It took me three days just thinking about what had happened. I couldn't shake off the feeling of the moments he spoke with us. On the third day, I realized it was an angel. Amid my despair, his words pierced my sadness and made me feel better. If God can send his angels to do that, how much more can we as humans, use kind words to others to change their feelings and their moments of despair. We can become hope, during their darkness!

My mom was that way. When I was down, she always looked for something good to say in the middle of my despair. I remember when I turned thirty-three. Mom knew it had been a tough year, financially and otherwise. She sent me a little Sunday school pamphlet in my birthday card, where she marked a passage about Jesus when He was thirty-three. It talked about how He went through the hardest years of His life, even to the point of dying on the cross, and yet it turned out for the very best. She knew I needed to hear that and that I would be okay too. She pulled me from despair! If I was down, she pointed out reasons I should be up, just as a real angel would do!

CHAPTER 4
Bobby Pins and Pin Curls

A lot of things went on in my mother's kitchen. When I was in first grade, my dad worked with my uncle and a friend from church as a second job. We lived in the camp house and together, his friend and brother-In-law, began to build houses in our small town. Dad got some great carpentry skills during this time, so he bought his land in our small town and together they all built our first home.

Dad designed it to fit Mom's taste! Pink brick and a pink bathroom with pink sinks. There was a long pink brick planter under Mom's big picture window. Her kitchen had an island with her sink facing the dining area. We had a big yellow table with yellow chairs that would seat six to eight people. In the dining area, Dad put another big window, so you could see the backyard. Mom loved her space!

I have so many memories in that kitchen! One that first made me laugh was the perms that took place in that kitchen! Back in the time when I was young everyone pretty much did their own perms, or the ladies did it for each other. It also seemed everyone had to perm their hair! So, Mom was going to give me a perm. I really didn't want one but that didn't matter! You had to get one!

Now if you don't know what a pin curl is, you take a small strand of hair, wrap it around your finger till it's tight to your head, then you put a bobby pin through it. You do this all over your head and when it dries, you have curls. Now Mom put perm solution in those pin curls and the pin curls just sprang back to my head when I pulled them out! I was devastated! I just cried and cried! I survived the embarrassment but would never let Mom give me another perm.

I was so thrilled when the neighbor built a beauty shop right by our backyard. The entrance was next to our fence. I had all my future cuts and styles done by her.

The owner of the shop had a daughter named Jean, who was near my age. We spent a lot of time playing basketball and playing monopoly together. Now Mom and her mom, Grandma Mills, did a lot of canning. Their dill pickles were the best! Jean and I developed a love for dill pickle sandwiches. All it was, was mayonnaise and dill pickles! I remember Mom was so upset when we ate all the dill pickles!

Another friend I spent lots of time with was Katy. She lived a few blocks away, and I'm sure we left a path between our houses. She lived with her mom and two brothers while her dad worked far away. Her mom was very strict and kept her on a tight leash! We were country girls. Katy was a true redhead! Her hair was long and wavy! We got in bad trouble for playing at the frog pond searching for tadpoles and getting muddy and dirty. We used the top of a shed at her house for a playhouse. Her big house had a long porch. We had a friend named Kathy and the three of us ran out of the screened kitchen door to play. Katy of course being first, jumped off the porch onto the bottom step as we all ran out the kitchen door.

Suddenly the rattling of a huge rattlesnake started, and I've never seen a redhead jump so high and go so far! She landed about six feet out! I froze, looking down at the snake and at my friend who kept running till she got to a tractor a full block down the road and flagged the man.

Her mom yelled at Kathy and I to come inside. The snake was gone when the man came, and we never found it. Ever since that moment, snakes are something I've highly respected. I'm always alert and have had to kill one rattler since then myself! It helped me overcome my fear.

Katy loved to come to Mom's kitchen. Her favorite thing was the sprayer on Mom's sink. Mom always told us not to play with it. One day, while Mom was washing dishes, Katy's busy hands hit the sprayer and Mom got wet! Growing up with Katy was always an adventure. We remain friends today but have lived apart.

Mom also taught me how to iron in that kitchen. I had a couple of scars to prove it. I learned quickly to respect the iron! Mom kept her sewing machine right on the dining room wall. She made many of my clothes, in my younger years. She loved to sew and helped me learn to sew on her machine. Often, the women at church would sew together. I have a quilt on my wall, signed by many of those church ladies, including my grandmothers. I came into that kitchen and dining room door, that joined our garage, every day after school.

As well as good memories in that kitchen, I also remember some not so good memories. I walked through the doors one day and there was Mom, crying her eyes out! Her brother, Alvie, had been hit by a train and killed. They were close in age and Mom was devastated!

Often, she told me the story of him and her being in school together. They had the same teacher. Alvie was a little mischievous and had gotten in trouble with the teacher. I could tell Mom thought it was funny, but the teacher put Alvie in the closet. So, Mom said Alvie pulled her fur coat down and stomped it.
She loved Alvie so much and losing him took a toll on her.

It was also after Mom's seizures started, that we came home one day to find her in terrible shape. She showed up at the door with a tennis-ball-sized knot on her forehead and more bruises as well. I thought someone had broken into our home and attacked her. She said she must have gone into a seizure on the couch which had wooden ends, just the size of the knot on her head. She looked like someone had beat her badly while we were gone. Fortunately, she did recover with time from that horrible episode!

Some of the other things I remember are walking through those doors and seeing the Beatles on television for the first time. I also remember seeing the pictures of President Kennedy being assassinated.

I remember being in Mom's kitchen one day. It was some time after Dad had come home after having his stroke. I had thought he was ready to drive so he drove to the post office to get their mail. I was working in the kitchen when he got back. I heard the automatic garage door open and heard Dad pull in. Then the door went back down, and Dad walked into the kitchen. I realized I could hear the car still running because he forgot he was supposed to turn the ignition off. I knew then he still had some healing time to go before he fully recovered from the major stroke.

Mom had a two-door copper tone ice box in that kitchen. On her icebox, she had a magnet that was sewn with mesh that said "Jesus." Later, after I was planning to move them close to me near Corpus Christi, a strange thing happened. I was in real estate and I often sold on the lake. I wanted to move them out of their two homes into one home. Since they had a lake home and the house Dad helped build, I had to find the perfect home on the water, so I could get them to move from two houses to one. I had run across a brick house with a metal roof. (Dad had put a metal roof on the hometown house). I went inside to look at the house and, in the kitchen, was a two-door copper tone ice box and on it was the magnetic "Jesus" sticker! Dad and Mom came down the next day, put an offer on the house, and bought it.

Now my God cares about the little things! He is a God that gives signs and wonders to all who will recognize Him for who He is! I call these wonders "God's Little World!" Many times, I stand amazed in His presence!

Mom's new kitchen at the lake had four pantries! She had two houses to move things from and she hated parting with her things, so she enjoyed her new kitchen.

I still see my first born in his blue bathtub, in her old kitchen, smiling from ear to ear on Mom's island in her kitchen as I was bathing him. Both of our sons are miracle babies! Our first born, Bryan, was our baby who we longed for during our childless years. As I mentioned previously, we thought after many months of trying, we would not be able to have children. We were at the point of both being tested to see what the problem was. I was praying God would give us a child.

It was the desire of my heart to be a mother! One night as I lay in bed, I heard God say, "You're going to have a baby!" I was so excited, I woke Mike up and told him, "God just told me that we are going to have a baby!"

It happened! A few months later, Bryan was born! Eighteen months later, Kevin was born!

We thought everything was good with him, but suddenly as an infant, he went into seizures. We called 911 and I gave him mouth to mouth. We rushed him to the emergency room where they took him quickly from me. That night he went into seizures five times. I stood outside his door, praying I would not lose my baby!

They ruled out spinal meningitis. They diagnosed him with fever seizures. Later, due to the fact he wouldn't eat, they tested him for cystic fibrosis. The first test was positive, but they wanted to test him again to be sure. I carried him to church with me on a Wednesday night. I taught the young girls, so after service I rushed him out to my Pastor and asked him to pray for Kevin. He laid hands on him and prayed. The next day he began eating. We had him retested and the test came back negative. God is so good! I give Him all the glory for giving us our sons. They were and are dedicated to Him! Mom was my guiding light, and I thank God that she introduced me to a Savior who always would be in control of my life! My mom's name was Oweta, and I am honored to share our lives with you!

CHAPTER 5
Let the Moves Begin!

Dad and Mom were excited to finally get the new lake house down by us. We were about thirty miles from them, but we knew I could care for them from there. Certainly, we had to find new doctors, but the move was very necessary for us, so I could be near to help them. We didn't have either of their houses sold, but Dad paid cash for the house near us and got a good deal. They simply had to get here, so all of us got together to get them packed and moved. I don't remember a lot about that time, but somehow moving time came, and we loaded up two houses worth of their belongings and my two brothers and I, and our families, moved them to Lake Corpus Christi. With the loaded rental truck, two houses full of furniture and a multitude of cars, we caravaned to Lake Corpus Christi! Working together as a family, we got them there!

Their house was on Lake Corpus Christi and there were some beautiful sunsets right out their back door. They loved the house and I loved having them down here. Dad had a fishing pier and dock to tie his boat up to. I think it took us almost two years, but we finally sold their other two houses.

Dad was getting a second chance at life after the stroke, and Mom would get a more modern house on the lake with her kitchen overlooking the water. I made many trips back and forth from Corpus Christi, as we found new doctors and had lots of doctor visits with their health issues. It wasn't too long till we were told that Dad's kidneys were beginning to fail him and very soon he would need dialysis. That changed everything! Mom didn't drive, and someone had to take him to dialysis four times a week. He had to do his dialysis in Corpus Christi, TX which was where I lived at the time. Dialysis day finally came, and we began. I had to drive thirty miles to get Dad and thirty miles to take him back and wait three hours for his treatments to be over. That was four days a week, meanwhile leaving Mom home alone with the potential of her having a seizure. It began to take its toll, so we knew we had to move closer to them.

We decided right away to try and move, so we put the house on the market. I was still showing houses on the lake during this time too, so I was on the road a lot! I remember showing an older home in Mathis to some clients. It was a 1942 home and I always loved the older homes! This home was priced way above our budget, so I remember showing it and seeing so much potential in the house. My clients didn't choose to buy it, but later this house will come into play in my story.

To my astonishment we got a contract quickly on our house and the buyers had cash money. They wanted us out in two weeks! I was going to do my best to make things happen, but I had to pack my house and find a house to move to. As a realtor I pulled a lot of rabbits out of the hat, but this one was a lot for me to comprehend!

I was packing as fast as I could, and I was looking for a place to move. I remember we found a house in the town near them that we thought we could afford, so we made an appointment to go see it. The house was horrible, and I could not see that house as even a possibility! It needed major remodeling. I'm talking about moving walls, sheet rock and it wasn't in a neighborhood where I wanted to live.

We knew we had little time and as I was praying about the big 1942 home, I was having thoughts that said, "God, I sure wish we could afford that house. I loved it and the fixes on it were something I could do."

Then the thought came to me. "I wonder if he would do a rent-purchase on the home?" It needed a lot of things done to it and with my real estate commissions, I could paint, tear out carpets, have new carpet installed and so on across the course of the next year. I would be improving his home and closing the house at the end of the following year.

The house was so much bigger than mine, I didn't even have enough furniture to fill it. I decided to approach the listing agent with my idea, so she could present my request to the owner. I called his agent and to my surprise, she called me back and said he was willing to do it. So, we got the contract going and I kept packing my house.

We were feeling so blessed and knew God was leading us in this move. I have to say, I didn't make it out of our house in two weeks! I think it took me three weeks to get out and to my surprise, I was packing and received a call from his real estate agent.

She said, "My buyer asked me to contact you and see if you would mind if he left

most of the furnishings in the house?"
Remember, we were short on furnishings
for this house. I said, "Yes, I think so!"

She said, "He wants you to come over and
go through the house. He will put a red dot
on the things he is taking and for you to
approve all the things he is leaving.

We did that! He had a red dot on an antique
piece and a dot on a picture to my
recollection. I asked, "Why doesn't he want
his stuff?"

She said that his wife had died, and they
had a house almost like this one on the lake.
He was moving there and didn't need
anything there. So, we moved into a fully
furnished house! With furniture from two
houses, I had my work cut out for me!

He had big dogs, and the Broyhill furniture
in the den and his white couch in the living
room was impossible to clean up. They had
to be trashed! However, he left some great
furnishings which included end tables,

coffee tables, a beautiful bedroom set and a huge dining room table with a hutch. These were very suited for the older style home and I loved the custom-made curtains. They were smoked damaged from chronic smoking and I was able to clean them and keep them. We painted, put new carpets down and we were on with our plan!

We had a very inexpensive rent for a year, then as planned, we closed on the house right on time.

Going through things there was like a treasure hunt. The house had a lot of history and the attic was full of Christmas treasures and decorations which I have used throughout the years. I was two miles from Dad and Mom and near the lake where most of my real estate business was. For the next two years, I would be highly active in caring for Dad and Mom and helping them through their last years! It was during this time that real estate took a big crash and my showings slowed down a lot. In a way, that was God's timing to allow me more time to care for Dad and Mom and be very involved in Dad's treatments.

We were so excited to learn that Dad might be a candidate for peritoneal dialysis at home. He was having problems with them hitting a vein, and the treatments were so hard on him. They had to put a stint in him, near his heart, to do his dialysis and we had the procedure done. Shortly after, I thought he would bleed to death in the emergency room due to the stint not being properly done. This mistake would be our great sadness that would later take his life, but at first, we thought we had everything moving right along!

To do dialysis at home, you must have someone do it for you or you must do it yourself. My dad's hands were totally messed up, due to his arthritis. His was a crippling arthritis that bent his fingers sideways. Although he did everything else with those hands, the dialysis was too tedious to do, so someone would need to do it and I would be that someone! He was my dad and I would have done anything for him to keep him here with me if I could. This would also allow us to be home with Mom. I knew, in volunteering to do this, I too would be homebound for as long as he lived, but I didn't mind!

We went to several weeks of training to learn the hook ups and soon we were on our way. Before that, Dad had been so weak, he had to use a rider in Walmart and other stores to get around. After training, all the supplies were shipped to his house and we would do his dialysis three times a week. We could do his dialysis right in front of his view of the lake sunsets. He could stare at the water and did not have to endure any more needles!

I was amazed! I took him to Walmart and let my husband and him out at the front door, then went to park. I went into the store and asked Mike, "Where did Dad go?" He said, "He took off walking in the store."

His energy had skyrocketed, and suddenly in the next day or two, he couldn't even walk across the living room floor. We were devastated! Had he gotten an infection? What had happened?

We got him in as soon as we could and ended up at the heart doctor. They sent us to a very good heart doctor in Houston, Texas. He would tell us if Dad was a candidate for surgery. He wasn't. They sent us home with very little hope, for his physical recovery. Mom had gone to a hospice facility to stay till we returned home.

Time after that was short for Dad. He had a mitral valve regurgitation from the stint they put in months earlier and it took his life. So much more went on that I will not go into, but Dad died in our local nursing home when I took off to eat breakfast with Mike, my husband. I think he didn't want me there when he went, and God honored his wishes. Telling my sweet mom and breaking her heart was hard, but family was with her.

I must tell you one more story about her when we were driving to Corpus Christi, and taking Dad to dialysis while leaving Mom at home We had her a button to push if she needed help, and she was on a walker or in her automatic wheelchair at all times. Well, going into her kitchen to get something, she fell while we were at dialysis. Her pants hung on a knob on the cabinets, stopping her from a full force landing. By the time we arrived home, emergency paramedics were there. They laughed and said had her pants not caught her, she would have possibly been hurt badly.

God is so good to us, both in life and in death. We must know that things here on this earth are only temporary! Our heavenly home is eternal, and our heavenly bodies will be perfect with no more sickness or sorrow to come. That was how my mom saw life and that is how I want to see it too. Because He lives, I can face tomorrow!

CHAPTER 6
There Was Beauty in Her Simplicity

For the most part, my mom was a gentle woman. I would call her a meek woman. She had a spirit of fight in her, but it was usually when she was hurt, or felt someone had hurt someone she loved. I have inherited that protective spirit, and sometimes, that can get in the way.

I've been more of a fighter than Mom, because I often felt like it was up to me to defend or fight for someone or something I believe in, but my best success is when I have learned to back off and ask God to intervene and conquer the battle! The battle is not ours, but the Lord's. This is a principle my mom taught me from the word of God! It was not so much what she said, but what she did that impacted all our lives!

When I went through hard times in my marriage, Mom always got me to focus on the good things about my husband. She would speak to me in a way that showed how much she loved me and him. She didn't take sides. She wanted me to see the good in him and in others. Always remember this! Even when you are in a God-arranged relationship, things can happen that will challenge you!

She made everyone that loved her feel loved. She did get hurt easily and she was very cautious about letting people hurt her twice. Her trust in others was easily shattered, so she taught me to always put my trust in God.

At their last home, their neighbor, John, was a veteran and lived alone. He was a reclusive person and on medication for his depression and anxiety. Sometimes he would forget to take his medication. He had lived with his parents till they died. His mom was an alcoholic and he cared for her as much as he could. He missed the lady who had been his neighbor before Dad and Mom bought her house, and he didn't trust anyone. Her daughter had committed suicide in Dad and Mom's driveway and that haunted him.

He thought everyone was out to get him and take advantage of him. He was a yard person and loved his yard and his plants. My dad and Mom and all of us tried to be good to him, but he made it very hard on us. Dad and Mom shared a septic system with him. His parents and the lady that lived there before them, had put it in together. Occasionally it had things that went wrong, so Dad and John would work on it together.

Through some interaction with John, Dad decided one day to mow John's lawn between their houses, just as a neighborly gesture. John got furious! We kept loving on him, but Mom was angry that he yelled at Daddy! Still I kept trying to be a peacemaker, so they could get along.

At Christmas dinners John was all alone, so I went over to see if he would like to join us or have a plate lunch. I knocked, and no one answered, so I went home and wrote a note and put it on his door. Somehow, he didn't see it till days later.

As time went by, and we continued to invite him to interact with our family, John began to change. I remember by the last year of Dad and Mom's lives, John had taken a liking to coming over to the house and visiting with Mom. I guess more than I knew, because he says she was his angel and she is the one that impacted his life to accept Jesus. He would watch Christian TV with her and at times, he would clean out her ice box and he knew she loved root beer floats and he would often fix her one in the evenings.

He began to work better with Dad and things got much better. Dad came down with kidney failure and we did his dialysis at home towards the end. John would sometimes travel with us to doctor appointments for Dad, so he could help me with him, and he also trained to help me with Dad's dialysis, in case I had an emergency and couldn't do it.

Mom didn't let the things John did stop her from teaching him and telling him about Jesus. That love for Jesus is what won John over to our family and taught him he was loved by Jesus. I continue the journey to work with John and he tells us every night he prays for everyone in the family.

The septic system was illegally done. It was shared with Dad and Mom, so when we sold their house, we put him in his own septic. We had to move his water well to make the septic system legal, so it was quite expensive to take care of it all, but we felt it was the right thing to do. I was in real estate at the time and for our buyers to get a loan, it had to be done. We are still the only family John has any dealings with. Other than that, he is still a loner, but his faith in God is still there and he says it's all because of my mother.

Mom taught us the Beatitudes and the Ten Commandments when we were children. The principles of those passages affected all her children's lives. She read us Bible stories and she explained everything about God to us. He was her closest friend and she made that clear to us! We wanted Him to be our closest friend too.

My youngest brother loves teaching in detail about the Beatitudes. My oldest brother loved the excitement and joy my mom felt about Heaven and studies of prophecies. I have a ministry of compassion, believing that God can minister to all kinds of hurt, all kinds of pain, all kinds of issues of this life, that people find themselves getting caught up in. I believe that everyone has a past that made them who they are, and they need a Savior to make them who God intended for them to be! I love my brothers and although we don't see each other as often anymore, I have faith that Heaven will move all of us close to each other again and we will rejoice with family, loved ones, God the Father, God the Son and God the Holy Ghost someday on the other side!

I know that physical pain was the biggest hindrance that Mom had to deal with, yet I saw that during her pain, Jesus held her together! We never know how much someone we love is hurting! The pressures of this life are enough, without having physical sickness to go along with it.

Dad pretty much took care of everything for Mom. She just had to focus on getting well and that was hard for her. She felt so frustrated and embarrassed at the seizures that began late in her life. Getting in public and going into a seizure was tough. We were thankful that for the most part, they were petit mal seizures.

Mom preferred to stay at home as much as possible, but she loved going to church to worship God! She covered her pain with the joy of the Lord! I still see that sweet smile when she would talk about the Lord and about Heaven! She knew that nothing or nobody could take that away from her!

This week, as I am writing, is the week that Evangelist Billy Graham went to his heavenly home! I am inspired to write about my mom because I see she has a sweet compassion; but she has a burning fire for Jesus and for the lost, to be saved. A compassion, just as I see in the life of Billy Graham.

Mom didn't minister all around the world, but she loved those who did, and she was one of their biggest cheerleaders! There wasn't anything that excited her more than a Billy Graham crusade coming on the TV. She had to watch and tell everyone she knew about it! What a real message on Christianity Billy Graham taught. A message of simplicity with an impact that could totally change a lost and a dying world. My prayer is this:

God, get me back to the simplicity and power of Your gospel! Let me be a light to a lost and dying world by sharing the simple, powerful message You have placed in me! It's not about me or about how much I know or do, but it's about how much I care! God, take away all the pressure I feel to perform, and put me in Your shadow so all will see who You are and what You desire to do for others. As believers accept you, may they go on to tell others about you! Help us all to bow down to You and honor all that You do and love with an unconditional love as You have done for us! God, we love You and praise You! You are the key that will unlock the doors of sickness, sadness, hopelessness, addiction, abandonment, and loneliness. I pray for moms, dads and children, across this nation and the world, that they would be great inspirations to all they meet! Amen!

CHAPTER 7

As Mom Taught Us, God Didn't Make Any Junk!

lot has happened since my writing in this book stopped in Chapter 6. God often assigns me to special people, more one on one, than anything. I have sought God as to what I am supposed to do in my mission for Him. We look around us and we see all kinds of gifts that people have and use for the Lord's work. If we are not careful, we start to compare ourselves to others and build expectations into our lives, other than God's expectations in His special calling and gift He has put in us. Like I said, my mom was a simple person, and yet she impacted so many with her love! Others might have thought it odd that she never had to work. She was a stay-at-home mom and her career was being a wife and mother. And even though she was home a lot, God sent people into her home that she highly impacted with the love of God shining right where she was. God often gives us assignments, and one of my assignments was John.

Here is the continuation of my story of life with John. It hasn't always been a situation that was easy. You must understand who God called me to be, to understand how and why God drew me into feeling a responsibility to John. You see, I wanted to know John's story. I am curious as to why a person who is alone feels so threatened by the rest of us and hides away from the world and seems angry all the time. That was the first John I met.

I am a people person. I am a very loyal person to my family and my spouse. When I met John, I perceived he was locked up in sadness, and possibly, no one else would hammer on that thick door he closed. He was determined to keep others from his life. I am a persistent knocker in life, and I figured if I was patient enough with John, I would get him to come out of his locked-up world.

Well it has taken a few years and I guess I'm as close as I'll ever be to figuring John out. You see, due to my persistence, John at least shared his needs at times with us and we were able to continue helping him after Dad and Mom died. We had him over for Christmas and Thanksgiving dinners, even though he wasn't family. Every year, I had a stocking on the fireplace at our house for John, along with our family stockings. He would still struggle with his anxiety, but generally loved the food and family get-togethers.

For a man who isolated himself, he loved to talk, and he really had a funny sense of humor, making it even harder to figure out why he isolated himself. Because he talked non-stop and my husband is not a big talker, he often stayed in the kitchen and would rattle on after a meal and make up for all the silence he suffered from at home. He knew my husband, Mike, liked to watch his shows on TV. He picked up on the fact that his abundant talking got on Mike's nerves.

John was on limited income and so he struggled at tax time. To pay for his property taxes each year, he drove his red van into Corpus Christi and parked it at the beach and lived in it. He would get temporary jobs nearby to raise the money he needed. I tried to keep up with him and knew he had been gone for about a month. I became worried after I was unable to reach him by phone. I thought maybe something had happened to him, so I contacted the police to do a welfare check. I went to the house with the police and they broke in through the back door to see if foul play had happened to him. I thought maybe he had brought someone home with him and they took his car. Well, he wasn't there! That was the first time I'd been in his house. It was a mess inside, but I'll explain later.

Well the search for John began with the police getting involved. It took a while, but they found him. He was living in his van somewhere on the beach and working days at a temporary job place. He was a little agitated because he had expired tags on his van and got ticketed when the police finally found him. He blamed me, but I told him that's what you get for staying gone so long and not checking in. He appreciated that we cared.

As more years went by, the old van he drove quit and we suggested he buy our son's old car which he did. The car was not good for the highway, but it got him to the store and back and helped him meet his needs. Then as more time passed, that car quit on him and he did not have transportation. He didn't want to spend anything fixing it, even though my son was sure of the part he needed. I then became his transportation.

He was out in the yard one day and he got hundreds of fire ant bites on his legs. He didn't tell us. When I saw him, he was covered with blisters, and had given himself very poor medical treatment. It had gotten so bad on his foot, that eventually it led to an amputation of his big toe. I took him to San Antonio for the surgery at the veteran's hospital. He was upset and scared, but I dropped him off and did some things to fill in the time.

When I picked him up, he was very moved by what he saw. He had walked out and there was a young man with no legs. John had just lost a toe and his fear and disappointment turned into being thankful for what he had left. That was a big example to me on how we need to recognize the scripture. In:

(1 Thessalonians 5:16-18), that says, "16 Rejoice always, 17 pray continually, 18 give thanks in all circumstances; for this is God's will for you in Christ Jesus. "If we hang on to what is important in this life, we will be able

to focus on the good things in life and not on the bad things!

So, for several years now, I have been taking John to doctor appointments and to get his groceries. About eight months ago, he almost completely quit going to the store. He started losing weight, which I assumed that he was not eating very well. I would freeze meals and take him leftovers and he was ordering online a lot. He would tell me if he needed something from the store and I would take it to his door. About three months ago he called an ambulance to take him to the emergency room because he was so weak. This was after the veteran's hospital doctors thought he had leukemia and had sent him to a veteran doctor, who was a specialist, to see if he had it. The veteran specialist they sent him to, said he did not have leukemia and sent him back, stating he couldn't find anything wrong. John was getting weaker and weaker and no one knew why. His weight loss was about ten pounds a month.

One day he called me, and he was so weak and said, "Bev, I need you to bring me some food. I've been lying in bed for 2 days and I can't get up. I am very weak."

I left and went by to talk to our local paramedics and sent them out ahead of me to check on him. I went for food. I met them on the way out to his house and they had left him already. They checked his vitals and said he was just weak from not eating, but his vitals were ok. I went to his house with the food. For the first time since that day I went in with the police, I went inside. I found him lying on a mattress with no bedding. The bottom of the bed was on the floor. John had told me for quite a while that he was a hoarder. I had told him I would help him if he would let me, but he always told me no. That day, I realized how bad it had gotten! At least somewhat. I knew I had to try to get him some help!

I called Health and Human Services and they came out. Now I had to see that he had meals and he got a little stronger as he ate each day. He wasn't ready to go to the hospital. He was convinced Health and Human Services would help him after he made progress in his house. They told him to work on it and they would come back in a month. He was two weeks into the month, and little did I know, he had not been able to do anything. I went to take him food one day, thinking I would see progress and realized no progress had been made.

I told him, "John, I said I would help you get things cleaned up, if you will let me!"

I knew it was a massive undertaking, but he agreed and asked for more time and we began. I told him it would be like eating an elephant, one bite at a time.

We started the cleanup and it was then that I realized the extent of the problem. He had boxes and boxes of stuff that was new and still in the boxes. He was not only a hoarder, but a chronic shopper. For years he did without air, heat, a kitchen sink and used what little he had left to shop and order on-line through his computer. We had worked about four days into the cleanup. During that time, I would open a box and John would say, "Congratulations, Beverly Ross, you just won a brand new set of sheets," or whatever the item was or he would say, "Tell Michael Ross he just won a brand new set of shoes," or fill in the blank with what the item was. He was determined to send all of it out and box by box, he would tell me to give it away or put it in the "keep" pile.

In four days, I had helped him, maybe a total of eight hours. It was then I got the call.

"Beverly, I made it to my office chair, and I'm done! I need you to come out here. I can't go anywhere. I'm too weak."

I called 911 and they met me there. This time, they had to bring in the gurney and had we not worked the four days they would not have been able to get it in there. He was diagnosed as having cardiac failure and halo-flighted to Corpus Christi to the same hospital and the same emergency room doctor he had seen before. About two weeks before he had been left on a gurney in the hall all day long and that same doctor told him there was nothing wrong with him. This time, he was halo-flighted and told he was in cardiac failure. They ran a scan to find the blockage and there was none. Instead what they found was a large tumor on his liver. The doctor gave him the grave news. He was almost certain it was cancer. He also required two pints of blood. This all happened on Mar. 12, 2018.

The night John was taken into the emergency room, he had to be intubated, then four days later was extubated. Altogether he received seventeen pints of blood. After being moved to a nursing facility, John died April 4, 2018. He went to the pearly gates of Heaven to join his dad and mom and my dad and mom. I would have loved to see his face upon meeting them all!

The few days of consciousness John had left after being extubated, were spent helping John with the process of an upcoming death. Number one was reading scripture to calm him and talking about Heaven and what it would be like. Finding out his favorite scripture was the 23rd Psalm, I put it on the phone, and he quoted it along with the man who was reading it. We talked about his two favorite songs. One was "I'll Fly Away" and the other one was "In the Garden." He wanted those sung at his funeral.

John had no provisions for death, so through those few weeks, we worked on that, so I could continue the mission to get his house ready. I was left to plan a funeral, handle his estate as the executrix, and through the few weeks, I met friends from his past who did not know the John I knew. A John that traveled the world, lived a very happy family life, served in the US Air Force, cared for his loving parents till they died, and had an abundance of friends and a wonderful and seemingly happy past. His friends have been a blessing, even from a long distance and have shown love and respect to him. They had no idea his life had fallen so low and now understand too, why he had been avoiding visits when they came to town.

You never know what causes a person to fall so low, but what I do know is everybody needs someone to be there for them: To be the hands and feet of Jesus to help. My many thanks go out to our military honorary members, who came with all honors to the gravesite to honor John's life for serving. I also am thankful for my son, Kevin and his friends who arranged it!

One of my favorite scriptures in the Bible comes from (Luke 4:18) and is also found in *(Isaiah 61:1) in the Bible. It says:*

18 "The Spirit of the Lord is on me, because he has anointed me to proclaim good news to the poor. He has sent me to proclaim freedom for the prisoners and recovery of sight for the blind, to set the oppressed free, 19 to proclaim the year of the Lord's favor." This is the work of the ones who truly believe in the Lord Jesus Christ and want to carry on the work here on this earth.

We also can learn about how Jesus wants to use us to lead others to Him and how we can serve in the "body of Christ!" In:

(1 Corinthians 12:12-31) speaks about unity and diversity in the body of Christ. It says, "12 Just as a body, though one, has many parts, but all its many parts form one body, so it is with Christ. 13 For we were all baptized by one Spirit so as to form one

body—whether Jews or Gentiles, slave or free—and we were all given the one Spirit to drink. 14 Even so the body is not made up of one part but of many. 15 Now if the foot should say, "Because I am not a hand, I do not belong to the body," it would not for that reason stop being part of the body. 16 And if the ear should say, "Because I am not an eye, I do not belong to the body," it would not for that reason stop being part of the body. 17 If the whole body were an eye, where would the sense of hearing be? If the whole body were an ear, where would the sense of smell be? 18 But in fact God has placed the parts in the body, every one of them, just as he wanted them to be. 19 If they were all one part, where would the body be? 20 As it is, there are many parts, but one body. 21 The eye cannot say to the hand, "I don't need you!" And the head cannot say to the feet, "I don't need you!" 22 On the contrary, those parts of the body that seem to be weaker are indispensable,

23 and the parts that we think are less honorable we treat with special honor. And the parts that are unpresentable are treated with special modesty, 24 while our presentable parts need no special treatment. But God has put the body together, giving greater honor to the parts that lacked it, 25 so that there should be no division in the body, but that its parts should have equal concern for each other. 26 If one part suffers, every part suffers with it; if one part is honored, every part rejoices with it. 27 Now you are the body of Christ, and each one of you is a part of it. 28 And God has placed in the church first apostles, second prophets, third teachers, then miracles, then gifts of healing, of helping, of guidance, and of different kinds of tongues. 29 Are all apostles? Are all prophets? Are all teachers? Do all work miracles? 30 Do all have gifts of healing? Do all speak in tongues? Do all interpret? 31

Now eagerly desire the greater gifts. And
yet I will show you the most excellent way.

That is why I say, we must be His hands
and feet!

This passage may be confusing to you if
you've just read it, but I will summarize it as
this. Every piece of your body has a specific
function! Every piece is useful and
necessary for full use of the body, but some
things don't seem to be as needed as
others. Like John's toe for instance! It was
important to him, but without it he could
still function! And he did. Now that toe
might not be missed like he would have
missed a leg, but he did miss it.

People who say they love and serve God,
may have a very big assignment, while
others may seemingly have a small task to
do. But in God's eyes, all are just as
important! Like a hair on the head, we don't
even know it's missing when it's gone!
Whether you do much or whether you do

little for the body of Christ, you are still a part of the body, and you are important! I think that is one way to look at the scripture. Another way is that if you are taking on a part in fulfilling the gospel of Christ, you can be an influence like a heart is to a body. You can be life changing for someone. The body has many "members," or things that make it a body. I hope to be a part of the body of Christ that makes a difference, whether I'm a significant part, or just a small part. God doesn't see insignificance in us. He just wants us to bloom where we are planted! I say every part of the body, even every hair is important to God. After all, He knows every hair on your head!

(Luke 12:7) says, "7 Indeed, the very hairs of your head are all numbered. Don't be afraid; you are worth more than many sparrows."

Consider every human on this earth, whether in the womb or walking on the earth, or lying in a coma or sitting in a wheelchair, you are valuable to God! You are priceless in His eyes!

The night John died I was sitting up at the nursing home with him. He didn't know I was there as far as I could tell. I just felt he needed occasional sponge water because he was so dry. I was just sitting in a chair at the end of the bed resting from the weeks of stress when the hospice nurse came in.

She told me she had another patient call and just thought she would stop in since they knew his time was near. I know now, God sent her. She told me, "Beverly, it really is okay for you to go home and get some rest. You know, John has been alone for a long time and he just might be waiting for you to leave. He will be alright if you do."

I took her advice, gathered my things and left. A few hours later they called me and told me he was gone. Now you would have to have known John, to know the excitement he would have had, in seeing his angel and Savior coming to take him home! I went to the nursing home just to pay my respects. I expected his eyes to be closed! Instead, I saw them wide open with a little "John" grin on his face! I knew he had seen the Lord!

John left this earth and you know what? He didn't get to take a thing with him. Believe me, as I have spent weeks going through all the things in boxes John had, God has revealed this to me in a way I don't think anyone could understand. Stuff just doesn't mean as much to me as it did! I love being blessed in this life and I know God expects us to enjoy the gifts here on earth he has given us. I do enjoy all he has blessed me with. But more importantly, we must realize at that moment, when God calls us home, all we have that matters is Jesus! We will enjoy eternity with our loved ones and others who we have influenced for the cause of Christ. Consider making amends with friends or loved ones you have hurt.

If you haven't appreciated the priceless gifts that God has given you, start appreciating them. The gift of family and friends is an eternal gift if we all get to Heaven together! Be a shining light for all you come in touch with! Don't put your closest family members aside chasing your dreams. Give your life and dreams to God and ask Him what He intended for you to do with your life. Then ask yourself...Am I doing it? Remember it's time to see yourself through God's eyes because God didn't make any junk. Speak highly of his creation!

This sums up what my mom, Oweta, taught me! You are created with a plan and a purpose. Your "test" in this life, can become your "testimony." God wants to use your mess and out of it make a message. Some people have really messed up lives but that doesn't matter to God. He didn't create the mess! His arch enemy, Satan did! He is the only one who can clean up the mess! He is not mad at you but loves you unconditionally, no matter what you have done. You can accept him today in your life, by praying this prayer!

Father, I am a sinner and I no longer want to live in this life full of anguish and regret. Jesus, I ask You to forgive me of my sin and come into my heart today! I long to have a relationship with You! Show me how to live and help me read and understand Your word. Let my life be a testimony to others so they can also be in a relationship with You. Thank you, Jesus, for dying on the cross and sacrificing your life for me. I love You and look forward to spending eternity with You! Amen

Made in the USA
Middletown, DE
09 February 2022

60190185R00056